It Was Like Watching

It Was Like Watching

The Last Books

Danny Hayward
It Was Like Watching

For MV

('the constant combination of two opposite modes of reaction … the latest innovation in the sphere of emotional life')

something rosehued, is scattered around
on the cold, unexpectedly cold floor
at specific times,
something green
I miss you. I'm too tired to write poems.
I'm too tired to have
a clever idea.
As intimate as sex before sex
itself becomes a tired rehearsal
of merely conventional meanings,
when it is still an image of space.
'It's OK, I'm on the pill.'
I look out at the sky, I guess.
it's the largest possible space there is
less expensive than hotels
or waking in a room I
don't recognise
which are other ways of approaching this.
The sea is too steep now.
The stars cannot reach it. A rented
room at the top of it waits,
waiting, dreams of your arrival

A

Likenesses

It's not   unhealthy. Look at me
This bright, reflective
raised platform. Not a subway.
I'm pregnant on a train.
I look out at the sky, I guess
it's the largest possible space there (is
less expensive than hotels
or waking in a room I
don't recognise
which are other ways of approaching this.
A rented room at the top of it waits,
Lights shine from its
its absence of. weight
equal to mass times
I miss you. I'm too tired to write (
I'm too tired to have
a clever.
As intimate as sex before this
itself becomes a tired rehearsal of
conventional meaning. The sea is too steep now,
the stars cannot reach it,
the carriage we wait in, aches.

*

We talked about art as a means to escape our   selves, our different selves.
We talked about art

together, the intensity of it, falling into the sea,

One of them preferred a language of concealment, the other of violent self-harm.
We talked about art. That's why it was a conversation

We talked about art. (In your notebook you would write beautifully around the
corners, as if there was no end to the page)

'it is what displaces you from your self-ratifying subjectivity' 'I only very rarely
had access anymore to a felt experience of those things'

we opened the door to the sea. we went all the way together, all the way, and I
didn't understand a thing. The tears of René Crevel. The books read by Guy
Debord. By 1935 I was in despair at not being able to physically maintain myself
at that level

...

*

On the tube I change at Camden Town
<u>Supplication</u> by John Wieners. p. 42.

the teenage girl on a swing
looks at him, an Instagram
account on her phone
she's alone
and it's about 7 a.m.

the taste of red bull
in what could be the next sentence,
(I dream thousands
of syllables
to replace it
thousands of them
to replace them
(I ride the underground with my
(eyes closed
(in a White Volvo. I can be turned around and
(eyes open)

'I also very rarely had access anymore to a felt experience of those things'

—

'Only those who are truly identified with their own selves no longer
need fear. And only those who get rid of their fear are capable of loving
nonjudgmentally. The ultimate goal of all human endeavour is to live
one's own life'

*

when I see you as you are
nothing can hurt us
and nothing is despised
time runs in any direction
the words race into me
for the first time this
is my mind and boredom
and hurt are nothing
everything is alive
when I see you as you are
and when I see you as you are
everything is
good enough, even
me, even this

When I see you as you are
there is a light in me
the sun has fun
making shadows
and the plants like to grow
it's like I'd never written
a single word about you
everything is magnificent
desert tundra ocean
terrain steppe
cityscape suburb
landfill & littoral

      (eyes open) (eyes closed)
      (eyes open) (eyes closed)

—

I ran out towards the 16th district and the streets were cold and
the other two smoked and looked out of the window and

it was like watching dust falling from the sun in an almost empty room
where a body evokes a kind of synaesthesia and it's all so interlaced
with my memories of your body which I would so much like
to touch again and wish I would have said I like to touch
more often though I did not, because I was too afraid
at first of what you'd think or what it might have sounded like

empty and musical and strange, and because I didn't know

there were things we never got to say to one another
or only very briefly at the end but they should
have taken years though and it's all so interlaced
with everything we disagreed about, and
my thoughts about language, this thread of dis-
satisfaction that was always more important (to me

than anything actually to be communicated,
in sex as much as in politics. and even now
as a way of getting beneath the surface
of things (between buildings,
corbels, festoons, cartouches
denticulations of sham palaces
of Jimmy Choo outlets and Rolex outlets

with my memories of your body and of mine
and the things I never did which I would so much like
to do, or did only very briefly at the end,
and soon will be coming home with them   again

        beneath deserted surfaces
        of our own words and gestures
        beneath deserted surfaces,
        it is yet wholly perceptible

Like dust, like dust,
fallen from the sun
like dust, fallen from the sun

and nothing will distinguish us
but our own ability
to find this kind of hatred
beneath deserted surfaces

of our own words and gestures
because it runs through everything
this thread of imperceptible
displeasure, and impatience

it is a kind of garden,
deprived of all dimensions
and yet wholly perceptible
wherever we should meet it

in the absence of a language
it will dawn on everything
these stained grey and cream walls
and everything perceivable

and here is where we meet
the others who are like us
in the absence of a language
we wake up from a dream instead

Like dust, like dust,
fallen from the sun
like dust, fallen from the sun

and then I knew how to say it. at dusk tonight I felt this amazing freedom.
I ran out towards the 16th district and the streets were cold and almost empty
words which run away from you and yet how you remained exactly who you were.
It was like watching dust falling from the sun. In a way it only confirmed
for me my idea about language, as in, it is only what is underneath that is
important and the places of your body that evoke a kind of synaesthesia

in me because it's all so interlaced with specific memories run like this thread of
imperceptible displeasure, and impatience through the streets of everything
empty and musical and strange, like words which run away from you and yet remain.

At dusk tonight I felt this amazing freedom.

When I came to,
this understanding
I saw that they
could show me
in which direction to
(eyes open) (eyes closed)
(eyes open) (eyes closed)
I could feel it immediately
throughout my entire body

(I dreamt thousands
of syllables
to replace it
thousands of them
to replace them
(I ride the underground with my
(eyes closed
(in a White Volvo. I can be turned around and
(eyes open)

When I came to,
this understanding,
I could feel it immediately throughout
my entire body,

My poetry lacks
the warmth of yours,
but I know
by the slight footprints
left by your wings
in which direction
to travel (through
thousands of
these syllables
(desert ocean
tundra terrain

steppe suburb
landfill & littoral

(eyes open) (eyes closed)
(eyes open) (eyes closed)

there is no language that is slight enough to slip through the ankle tag,
no thought, no vaseline of thought. My poetry lacks the warmth of
    yours,
but I know by the slight footprints left by your wings in which
    direction to—

about 22% of this is real.

B

Dialogues

A: I write what I am not meant to think
       because it is beautiful
       even if
       it is intolerable
       I invent a fawn
       I no longer think I am
       one, I don't want to come back

       in time, all things become lakes, stars and mirrors:
       botched surgery between the rectum and the anus

       an explicit Instagram account

       belonging to the American fashion designer born in Fresno, California,
       working on a diffusion line for Ralph Lauren,

B: There is nothing I am not meant to think
       time plays with these human figures like keys
       gives them its sexually transmitted disease

C: Generally it's assumed the reader is non-infected an angel
       who spends their evenings reading the later poems of Paul Celan and, you
               know,
       their body is the starting point.

       More than anything I am interested in giving up

D:

well, it's a nightmare then, another dead end
, the court poets,
dependants of tyrants, habitués
of the advanced literary culture
of alexandria, could no longer
flesh out their anger and were reduced
to looking for bursts and flashes that would,

in any case there's this threshold that you
cannot cross, a point beyond which you find
myself, in endless, immutable motion,
the limit to this changeless sense in which
their body is always the starting point
it is no longer simply about writing it
I am what I am not meant to think.

—

E: I hate what I am not meant to think.
       To write poetry means changing everything
       without changing yourself
       The millions of neurons it takes to look out of the window
       are humiliated by what they are forced to see

dialogue between

1:

You are always obliterating me with your space

       When I position myself
behind you you cry out needlessly and your hands
      shake.

and you have nothing to show   anyone

If you would let me touch you
      you might yet become
what you wanted to
         be,
you would only have to cry out
      once, to the rhythm of events themselves

Because I mimic what you hate, I steal its
strength.

the feeling of submission and release is
a beautiful dance of   perception

                  understand,

                  I put my fingers into the gaps

of your vocabulary

                  and lick them

I am ready to endure

The dialogue between the soul and the body has nothing
on

2:

You don't even understand who I am.

You talk about diseases who have never had   a disease

When you come to my bedroom it has no doors and no windows,

it is beyond you.

When you touched my perineum and kissed me

I was an adult

but years have gone by and now

what you think of as my 'goodness' is nothing but my complete
absence from your

.

The rhythm of onrushing events does not move me
any more
        than your fingers   do

If you would let me touch you
you might yet become,

what you wanted to be

the argument

writes poems——from the perspective of——doesn't matter.——Musical notes.
Four hands & a——thin. from the. Perspective. I write from, the perspective of
——75 feet up in the air and——Don't matter. had——a relapse for whom this is
——impossible. I write from——of opposites, in the, same——poetry——it is
a perspective——Of. perspective. Doesn't——the perspective of——Hellas and
the burnt plain——Doesn't——its. sleeping rough in——your own, body——is
a dream of——is perspective of course——(Doesn't.)——'The old revolutionary
demand for a——'helpline'——of, the perspective of——from that which has.
never ceased to exist and which takes the place of——Doesn't——exist.——
perspective of——of——a——a number of. relapse lanterns'——that cannot be
——which takes the place, of——interiorised. O the burnt——of the, burnt for
whom——perspective, of——it is, of. 'lanterns'——from the(——your own)——
of, a——in the. Doesn't——'helplines'?——OF the enormous area of a, CD
——a CD of it——burnt——a——your Perspective 'doesn't'(——falling, in the
future——like the sun on the——of——the. perspective, of——impossible——
like, Doesn't matter.——I write from the, perspective of——you——don't——
write——for you whom——is——who never has. never——of the life that is——
itself. A whole area, in the air——is——from the. the perspective, of——I am,
not——at the limit, of. Don't. matter——bound and led towards or. nothing

C

Casualties

Like weary runners you return
to yourself each night with feet filthy and blistered
in your dark, excessively large flat
You read Paul Eluard, listen to New Order,
skim through *Advanced Trauma Life Support For Doctors*

A poet

Every day
they go to lie in slightly roasted grass on the Zionist
Uni Wien campus, on dry earth,
The grass yellowed like straw
silent, expectant
they lie flat on their stomach and look out.
    It is good and warm,
        and children are playing with other
            children, by the swings

by shifting the meaning of one word into another, they think
you can escape from thoughts into images
which communicate with each other in their own language
which has yet to be overtaken
by this endless counterinsurgency, the basic justification
of the endless killing
which is the way you continue to

      (there is something repulsive about this person, the overused word

      'artist' probably applies to them

they write poetry the way wind interacts with leaves
or the way that light slants vertically backwards across a wall,
in the way you perceive things to interact with one another.
they think this is the only way they can continue
the way pine needles fall, are crushed between fingers
releasing their unmistakable
scent

You grow tired
you produce an endless random interchange of the same images
your work is of little significance
it has violated
no laws, caused no harm,
has led to the discomfiture
of no enemy,
has not even grazed their face.

Another poet

conducts research,
          reads illegally downloaded
medical textbooks about sepsis
              late into the night

about the need for prompt dialysis, about how blood fails to move
as it should
in the smallest blood vessels.

they write a poem bordering on anti-Semitism
testing out a boundary
thinking the thing on the boundary is true

                they take their last three Xanax and close their eyes

                but all you see is a picture of someone's else's face
                destroyed in a car accident
                you get up and walk to the window they look at the wall

there are years that do not go by

                like sacks of dried goods, cassettes, coffee kettles, and prayer rugs

or the delicate organisation of
eyes and nose and mouth, do not care
for their endless faces

how we lay in June, on such a transparent summer morning

in a library of the Eighth District, they think it is possible to combine every

this may take several minutes $EtCO_2$

sepsis, a bacterial infection triggering an immune response

causing the release of small proteins, leading blood vessels to dilate

before they sleep they masturbate their poems, torn by
conflicting

impulses lose their

beautiful power to narrate the drop of blood pressure, leading to septic
shock, etc.

'the refusal to accept that which, deep within ourselves, we know to be true …
this is laughter, emanating
from a struggle that is internal
to ourselves

Or face down on a mattress, laughing,

in the literate superstructure, injected into the air

by a. nice night nurse called Tony—

wounds treated with fire without sympathy—

to form a skyline, deep within ourselves.

more than anything I am interested in giving up

on getting better.

I exchange you for that

truthless horizon, that implant,

this desire to improve. I am finding out what it is possible to do

here, I am seeing it right through to the end.

A poet

One night, from the window of a hotel in the Netherlands they look out at
    a carpark
the words 'fresh shallow sealight yellow'
flash up in their mind
they finger their asshole while looking at themselves in the mirror, go to sleep.

    a dream of things to come are
    and plastic bags
    and makeshift tombs

  there are

certain aspects of
your own life
you would rather not see they are
reflected in your
silence, in a way
that is shameful,
behind your listless
eyes you feel
the intensest parts of your life
are so huge
and so forceful
there is no
place for them
in this empty

One night, from the window of a hotel in the Netherlands they look out at
     a carpark
the words 'fresh sallow yellow sealit'
flash up in their mind
they invent new words while looking at themselves in the mirror, go to sleep.

They grow tired
produce an endless…

Another poet

Your poems are so quiet

Another poet

they sit in a cafe on a canal

     In front of them a book by Josef Albers

          to read at a scratched plasticated table   We are going by in the
               street outside

(I lost consciousness of Idyll LXI,
its images scabbed over like the iced-over pond of Rege—

'When you come to my bedroom it has no doors and no windows,

it is beyond you.

When you touched my

still, but years have gone by and

their words are so much smoother and clearer now

—

'She continued to read Lorca, whom she admired greatly, in Hebrew for the rest
of her life.'

I await an unknown thing, or perhaps not knowing the mystery and your cries,
you scatter the last bruised tears of a childhood like cold precious stones that
detach themselves from the eyes, illuminating their own purpose

Another poet

writes poems bright as a candle

    which make people laugh

    with their endless tangle of lips and limbs

and glancing contemporary allusions,

brief and perfect for

They do not exist

You are that poet

    You know that poetry is
    just something an LA industry plant with a father who has sexually assaulted

doors

that never appears as such,

invented

Two years later you begin to
explore brittleness, changes in colour,
everything that flakes, sags and weeps
is known to you
You write openly
about sex and desire
They are a huge part of your life and you should
do
this though things do not appear as themselves
Your poems are slightly less sexually explicit than
and slightly less witty than

> later you come to think that a poem is a place to change sex, kill
> someone,
> depict a room with nothing outside of it,
>
> say the opposite of what you think
>
> you contract poetry, '
>
> Imagine yourself as a sad little balloon
> floating high over a deep wet sea
>
> your poems become darker, crueller.
> Before you die of poetry in 1991,

you publish your final book, 'I will escape from everything you say and everything
you think'

in which nakedness is a balloon carried by a little boy
who learns there is no such thing as touch
and that communication is impossible

in your last poems, no such thing is impossible
as there is no such thing,

toothless, mean-spirited provocations, saturnine and saturated with an

[37]

already your name is being forgotten,

and other poets appear to take your place

Here and there

Astonishing and heartbreaking swellings
appear in your language,
seeming to have no correspondence to words as they
exist or are spoken
by

another poet,

they are tired, they write

Ich glaub', das ist der Teufel,
Ja, ja, das ist der Teufel,
Ach, wär ich eine Maus,
Wie wollt' ich mich verstecken,
Ach, wär ich eine Schnecken,
Gleich kröch ich in mein Haus

another poet,

they are tired, they write

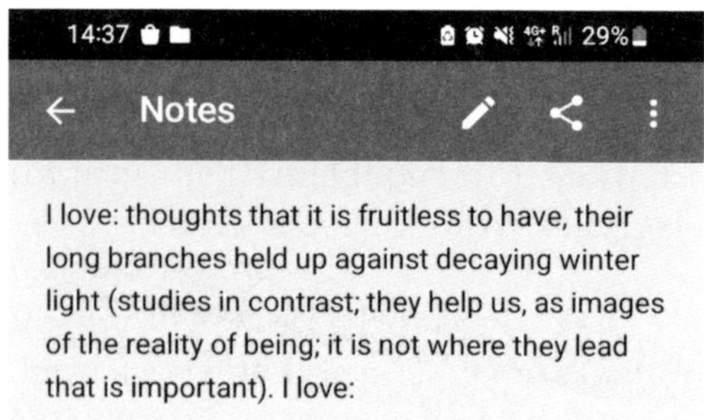

[38]

I love: the small square of blue above the roofs.
To return in the end to the same point at which
we begin.

I love: The little boy who gouges out cats' eyes,
the little girl who dismembers her dolls.

I love: the street corner; a lake or a puddle; a
cloud that provides the water I need.

I love: to keep my eyes wide open, as I have done
up until now, so often in the course of my life.
"There can be no geniuses except among men
affected by some fury".

I love: that I am still here, in spite of everything,
that I am still here and that I am able to perceive
(if this is what perception is), and I love that
there are others who are with me, for now, for
this, for the moment, for today, for a little while,
still, in spite of everything.

***

III   O   ‹

another poet

I feel sick of this,
hate the mere act of invention
the intense parts of my life
are so huge
so forceful,

when you were still there,

why is it that I need to take this step back

    to invent all these paper-thin characters

[39]

the intense parts of my life
(burn perspective away

I feel sick of this,
hate the mere act of pretense
they burn perspective away,
for months
before I
began this
I saw this poetry as

(stable perspective, deferents, epicycles)

a journey through

(stable perspective, deferents)

I began this
(a year now
(a naked
stable perspective
, each
coloured by other events
other modes,
impulses

I wrote a poem then.

I feel sick of this
saw poetry escape,
a journey begins
with nakedness, being alone
hating the vanity of pretense
(I feel sick of this,
the vain acts of my life
burn pretense away
so many acts of pretense)

I feel sick of this

I begin, there is no
place for this,
for subtle shifts and changes of
(poems written by

poems, written
by different
perspectives
burn perspective away
(anxiously pulling my dress (down
(a journey to
(with no
beginning
(with
nakedness,
ends with

I felt sick of this
I began
saw poetry escape into
images of an explicit
Instagram account,
a naked bathroom selfie.
I will follow it

it will follow
(me
poems are written
hating the vain enjoyment of pretense
it is a journey
with no end no beginning

why I burn perspective away
anxiously pulling my dress down

in late August I met one of your friends

we travelled together on the bus
I was

helping her with directions, looking at her phone, on her lap and she
anxiously pulled her dress down

I don't know whether it's just because I
I feel sick of
this, subtle shifts of pers
pective
having to hate the journey with
no end

but the image stuck

I will begin this now.
It is not important,
my willing
ness to
give you
(the problem of
my life,
(to follow it where
ever they go,

burn perspective away
'perspective' is
only images, an explicit
Instagram
account

there is no
place for them in what I write
only
for subtle shifts and changes.

I begin this now.
'nakedness'
is)
poems written by
different poets
are my nakedness

the
way I burn
perspective down

I begin this now
I feel sick I will begin this
with no end, no beginning
a sense of nakedness
(of being alone
in the bathroom mirror
is not perspective,
is only

I begin this now
two months
ago
a naked bathroom selfie
I never did,
hating the journey with
no end
anxiously pulling my (dress) down

I begin this,
now to feel sick I will begin this
with no end (and no beginning
to my nakedness,
of being alone
in the bathroom mirror
it is not a journey through
it is only

a perception

I begin this now
I saw poetry escape
into you, the intensest parts of my life

burn away

[43]

I begin this now
subtle shifts and changes
are journeys
with
out (
I begin this now
anxiously pulling my dress down
remembering you
who are
are the whole
of

I begin this now,
with my nakedness,
the loss of
self embarks
on journeys
without end

I begin this now
anxiously pulling my dress down
I am a (naked bathroom selfie
burns perspective
(away
you are, as I am
you will
as I am, the whole
of my,
as I am

(now I begin,
anxiously pulling my dress down,
a naked bathroom selfie
burns perspective away
the loss of my
self embarks
on journeys
without end

I feel sick of this
I begin now
with no perspective at
all
things
can run
into the opp
osite

begin this, now
begin
I feel sick today
because there is no end to this
no (
I will be
there with (the whole of my
through

I begin this (feeling this sick this now
I know there is no end,)
I know there is only a journey,
no perspective.
only poems
write poems
vain) vanity of pretense

I begin this
I know there is no end,
the directions I can take
can only be
reversed
(
a journey through

I begin this now,
a naked bathroom selfie
burns perspective away,
the intensest parts of my life

neither nor especially
new

(I feel sick of this, because (no end to this

I begin this now
I know there is no end to this
the directions I indicate
are only movements, between and within

I begin this now,
directions indicate
only movements, between and within,
different
movements,
journey through

I am a different poet then.

I begin this now
anxiously pulling my dress down
taking a bathroom mirror selfie
the whole burned perspective is burned away
I won't make the same mistakes again
The mistakes I made with you.
I know you are the whole of my   through.
I know that my   only
I know you are my   only

                    (White lights curve, it is raining
                    when desire comes, a bedroom appears without any effort
                    snow melts on the heights of Haemus etc
                    that is also a kind of strength,
                    even in its weakest form,

                    it is movement)

I begin this now

This is when absence and sorrow, and all the available
manifold for denying, mediating or pleating the actuality
of them, start to feel superfluous since indeed this is just
a short period of 'getting things done', of actively
cancelling the full if undefined quantum of terrors
(demands, strivings) which would otherwise impinge on
all this time that we will have together

another poet

they sit in a cafe on the canal

(you've seen this one already) In front of them a book by Josef Albers

      they read

a scratched plasticated table

a man watches them from near the counter

        They are tired. They are waiting for beauty to become plausible again.

      You [

Outside,

it is all blue as a vape. They look at their device—

Two verse lectures about the 'war', in lines which have thinned out to single letters,

others about how they had sex and then fell asleep

in one another's
arms,

belonging to the

line
running back through—

'the whole tradition of bucolic poetry'

      they wonder how they could have written all this,

what the connection is

                outside, though it is still summer
                soft, cold
                flakes remaining white

                do not melt,

                they fall, though the sun kisses the buildings—

                and the windows of houses, and the windows of hopes

(this is the nature of marvell's pastoral reference to a world: a pure ground,
a blank canvas on which he could paint his own imagined relationship to love
without the grotesque infiltration of a reality he could not otherwise hold at
arm's length, being in it,

the troopers enter his poem in its first line,

'the qualities themselves', writes Albers,

'were staircases, into crumpled rain, so we ran up them and the buildings tumbled
in on themselves'. ('So long as we hear merely single tones we do not hear

music.'

they think

there is no way actually to live like this,

the incredible simplicity of a direct relation, that my mind feels clear and the
writing is here in the way another person is.

it is only when you see what has been destroyed that you can know what
destruction is

—

AND on this night when I finally realised
that there was no way back
and I had nothing to say,
in the back of a car, in this six-seater taxi with the radio
on and the Avril Lavigne club remixes
plunging into the night,
in the back of this car, with the radio
on and Avril Lavigne club remixes,
plunging ever further into
the night, ever deeper into representation
on this night

    Two seasons have passed, the whole summer
    and the first part
    of spring. I lay on the grass,
    and what I learn is
    really simple:

    tonight I sit in our living room and look at the front door. I only do that.

    (The mind
    is different,
    but the
    same—

    it's the way likenesses here always seem to mean pain and you can never
    really get
    free of
    them,

because the
likeness itself is in the likeness of meaning and so however much you just
want to show
some
thing,

this is how I persuade myself to repeat your words,
to touch them
with
my mind and taste them and push them into my mouth, never really knowing

why

they taste so much like the cold on your cheeks when you came in, on
what
I continue
to call
yester
day

it is there

but feelings change and I want to move with you through difference, no
matter

where

touching one another in the stranger's plaster
board
hall
near
their front
door,
never

really knowing why

the lawn,

(you were broke then and alone, trying to figure out what it is you wanted
and
why
it was there, this feeling
of
what
I continue

to call

,

remembering nothing but endless fucking and smoking weed in Deptford
wondering
if you ever really did feel it, (
never
really
knowing

why

lawn

never really knowing why

sometimes, the mind is just another way of touching, a similarity without
difference, in
which
your (
resemble

(later,
you would always say South London has this particular sub

urban

feeling

of

space for you

and I realise
now how
that was
fixed in
place
for you

this

grass
I push into
my mouth,

this likeness

…

AND on this night when I finally realised
that there was no way back
and I had nothing to say,
in the back of a car, in this six-seater taxi with the radio
on and the Avril Lavigne club remixes
plunging into the night,
in the back of this car, with the radio
on and Avril Lavigne club remixes
plunging ever further into
the night, ever deeper into representation
on this night
when you felt alive and when I felt dead
and on that night when I finally realised
that there is no way back
and I had nothing to say,
in the back of the car, this six-seater taxi with the radio
on, and the Avril Lavigne club remixes
plunging into the night
in the back of the car, with the radio

on, and the Avril Lavigne club remixes
moving ever further into
representation
ever further in
on this night, when I felt alive and when I felt dead
on this night when I finally realised
there is no way back
and I had nothing to say,
literally nothing to say about, like
(but you know nothing about my life)
in this six-seater taxi with the radio on
and the Avril Lavigne club remixes
and our knees pressed together—
but I don't—
I don't remember, I'm just making things up—
in the back of this car, this six-seater with the radio
on, on that night when I finally realised
what it feels like,
on that night when I finally realised,
in the taxi with the Avril Lavigne club remixes

,
scrolling right like prices, in red dots
(where my sweet fawn is vanish'd to /
Wither the doves and turtles go)

On this night when I finally realised,
in the back of this car, the six-seater with the radio on,
trying to bring the phrases back into the active area of my life
where things ebb and flow
and are

I always believed

    if you use your mouth it doesn't count, right
    I wanted to make it sound so gentle,
    so naive, what if we just do it with our mouths
    (there's still all of these beautiful lights,

    what if the images drive us through a language

we no longer resemble
like a chauffeur,
our thoughts in the back
(the image that can still be imagined
is paid not to look,
like a chauffeur
(eyes open) (eyes closed)
what if we made it so gentle
we don't
even have mouths anymore we don't even
touch anymore what if
we don't
even have eyes anymore what if
one of us isn't even here anymore
and it's impossible to imagine
what we do anymore, in these beautiful lights
what if we drive through a language
we used to resemble and don't even
speak
anymore, our thoughts in the back
don't have mouths anymore and (eyes open)
what if they don't even touch
anymore
which cannot

does it count

on this night when I finally realised,
all things are paintings of themselves
in which things greater than themselves are born
and born again, endlessly, and stars
are mirrors of themselves, and greater things
are born again, endlessly, as mirrors
of things, greater than themselves
I did not close your eyes, but they stay open.
There were still all of these beautiful lights
and our knees are still pressed together.

(… I did not close your eyes—they stay open and overwhelming
lights in a rearview mirror that cannot be imagined though
I can resemble it, or pay someone else not to look. there's always
someone else you can pay not to look, in infinite variations:
The image as a chauffeur through what are we waiting for,
through what we are waiting for, through what are we for.
I did not close your eyes, but they stay open. This notebook is full.)

Another poet

She strolls out into the street,

where a scaffold is enwrapped in flames. It is her last years of wandering. She
reads and embraces the new

poetry   the 'I' a dead blind seer jiggling his snake-like titties, a sequin, tossed into

breakwaters

she moves to Hawaii, kneels down in the cold surf

> They still use words like 'poem' in their poems and 'word',
> When others complain they write
> 'Reality does not care about your complex or simple
> It is extremely crude when you are poor:
> life is worthless and there is
> always worse to come.'

In their most beautiful poem you see a motorway leading to an airport at dusk,
a simple flow of light, steady and uninterrupted. A warehouse, static, unchanging.
The colour of an unspeakable room, where they show to you what doesn't even
exist, is always half of itself, a hell of itself, that my mind is always half of itself,
a hell of itself, and it's like… it's…

Two years later, after they've published their last book,

[55]

They'll sit by a river in a city where you were not born.
Huge swans fly in groups to and fro—
the determination of their long white forms.

The river is somehow the most solid thing there is,
endlessly more solid than the crumbling city that surrounds it,
an emptiness of trees and of night.

When they die, their last Google search will be 'actor 50 dead drug overdose'
and when you look at their notebook,
the last lines they will have written will be
'my thoughts have become stiff, like a once famous actor, dead of a drug overdose
at 50'

another poet

writes poems describing   killings, long lists, descriptions of
forensic, unsparing.

Lenin failed. And so did Brecht. And so did you. And so do I.

another poet

writes a poem

in their most violent poem a. You will say anything to get a reaction.

while saying absolutely nothing

('through the window, on each side,
one could distinguish a colorless, pale sun,
tainted by large black spots,
with a little more light in the center')

Another poet

Says nothing. thinks about another poet thirsting after teenage boys in the
impossible daytime sunlight, a sunlight that exists only in his imagination,
dreamed, invented, just like the boys themselves,

who are only the shepherds, clowns, figures in the Idylls of—some
unreconstructed bigot.
And the other poet is also dreamed, invented. because that's what it means to

endure

and now I'm thinking of a long stretch of empty time, the time of searching
and not finding,
where the faculties fly over barren distances, seekers of some asymmetrical qualities
of themselves

But then you also wrote 'I also very rarely had access anymore to a felt experience
of those things'

and I understood this to mean that I could also begin here: that the deprivation
of love or anything else, security, conviction, even the idea of a self, as something
other than this endless series of feints, could be a means, an organising constraint,
as they already are, for most people

who aren't filled with inadequate leftist jargon, or whatever, but really, that's not
the point. I thought of deprivation as a means, an organising constraint, the point
of deprivation as the point of beginning, where something that has been taken
from you is turned back on itself and becomes pure empty space through which
something else moves,

but that's just the obvious idea about negativity, or absence; you know it already:
'Now my sweet fawn is vanish'd to Whither the swans and turtles go'.

and arms that poison earth will show
the future who we really are

[…]

Another poet

cries and pulls their baseball cap over their eyes.

     their young language reflects their great strength

        even when it comes out wrong,

     even when it is specked with mud, or assaultive, or [......]

        Barcelona Reus, Paris Beauvais

I dream thousands
of syllables
to replace it
thousands of them

Barcelona Reus, Paris Beauvais'

... and even when it starts to lose its focus on reality
     and drivels on about the way wind interacts with leaves
        or the way that light slants vertically backwards across a wall

     there's something in it. It's a language that feels good somehow, and
somehow different to

everything else

     everything else that exists

and because it is this and what it is and nothing else without ever apologising

and because all impulses simply appear in it, just like that,

        as though it were saying
           sorry to everything which doesn't exist

anymore, even when it doesn't exist anymore, even in memory and this image of a

[58]

young poet at a

reading in minimal

sportswear   pulled out of its

BMW, retching   persists all the way to the end and even

                 when they are actually a fascist   even when they try with desperate

acts of aggression to revive something

and you don't want to read them anymore because it's all so dull and predictable

there's still something in their language that feels good somehow, and somehow
different to

everything

[…]

saying
                 I'm sorry,

                         being forgiven

                 […]

                 Barcelona Reus, Paris Beauvais,

I can't keep refocusing
it is something to do with the distances between breaths
snow, and salt and

As if the absolute nakedness of one human being to another

were anything more than bones keep turning up in their cheese.

We're running out of poets now.

This poet is colourless. Her words make
        terrible inroads into the hearts of her
                listeners. Her language is the language of a

person, as pastoral and innocent as our own
        unendurable consent. Evoking something
                beyond endurance, beyond secrecy

when she walks about, lilies grow in the heedless
        tread, of her feet. But some note
                that a spot of obscurity in her language

cannot be bleached, out. And yet her face is calm,
                framed by an exuberant potted plant
                        as airbrushed and flawless as a mannequin's.

In her last poem there is an image so heartbreaking,
                no one who reads can forget   it. It is an image
                of absolute freedom.

something, perhaps beauty, or the self, or desire
                is being put away. It is being placed
                        very carefully, into a kind of box

but the box is not meant for these things. Somehow
                it is a beautiful, desiring, speaking box,
                        and when you put beauty, or the self, or de-

sire into it, it will—but readers argue about
                    what happens next. That's part of the magic
                            a poem so breathtaking no one can forget

it. And then the focus shifts to something so obvious
                    that very few people noticed
                                was
                                        there all

another poet

You have become me,
but you did not see me

showing you my
self, like many other things that cannot be tasted or seen

when I was sad after the reading
        you leapt to me over time and memory and beauty

because we belong together
        and give one another an obscenity that is   the equal

to beguiling compassion. As you play with dissonances and harmonies I play
        with nakedness and repulsion.

You may think I represent abundance and happiness
but our shared propensity for misunderstanding is how we understood

Car ma facon de voir, apres tout.

Another poet

                            they are tired, they write

The only way to write a successful poem is,

you make someone else feel that they're not unique.

you address a specific fraction of them (I am beginning to find

(the tubes running from your nostrils can be removed, like (clothes (you are
     always there,

in the blue of the night in which we

survive our own thoughts,

as cold and simple as an ocean of screen,

with your mouth wide open, and mine pressed to yours.

        I have to live with that.

I have to live with that.

> And this is a fairytale story. the story of a child
> deprived of love, (of course)
>
> of a movement between two worlds, separated by
> an impassable
> (but I could no longer avoid the question of how
> much love that was, since even if my love should
> continue to grow now nothing would change)
>
> "Let us remember that Sodom was supposed to
> look like an Italian city in the fifties. It is as if in
> leaving Sodom the two pilgrims
> had also traveled in time".
>
> from each window, slightly wasted faces of children
> gaze down upon our procession.
>
> One day, there was a sea above the land and the sea.
> On top of it there was a rented room. every day the
> contents of the room would be different. One day it

[63]

would be full of light, tender rose grey threads, of
english words, evoking the bodies of

lovers, the next it would be full of weed smoke and
Playstation 2, and no   then a   decrepit cafe where
your young 'intellectual' friend buys you a glass of
bitter boiled tea,

in this place where everything changes,

you imagine travelling to a place where

everything counts. You play Fifa and smoke until
your eyes

One day, there was a sea above the land and the,
it had a rented room on top of it and each day
the room would be different. One day, it would
be like and then the next it would be like, um,

where for once we completely forgot ourselves

(Of wide expanses of water, moving, or still, or

Of a city whose centre is its circumference
(like something taking place in Malevich's head
and on the next a waiting room full of melted
plastic chairs, or
some basic epistemological failure

One day, a scary rain comes in, through the
window, to lead us away, bound and chained
from, towards Paradise. You pass a desolate
landscape made of "deserted villages" and "long
deserted roads." "On the horizon," we see "the
Pyrenees vaguely menacing, like an ashen wall."

through forest desert ocean tundra terrain steppe
cityscape suburb landfill & littoral,

and the journey takes about thirteen years. on the
last day you climb through a wire fence into a, um
whose window looks out along wide, otherwise
empty streets.

Paradise is finality, it is the place where everything
counts,

it is a fairytale story. Taken and carried ashore with
your hands Pinioned fast behind you to this place
where you did what you did, and loved what you
loved,

['I can't recognize myself anymore, because what
made me similar to other people has been
destroyed… You have made me different, by taking
me away from the normal course of things… To
know that I have to lose you has made me aware of
my diversity. What will happen to me in the future?
My future will be like living with someone, myself,
who has nothing to do with me.']

um. yeah. everything is visible here as an amount,
a sum and you know it will never change, because
what you did is what you did and what you loved
is what you loved   in this place where everything
is visible, is final because what you did is what you
did and what you loved is what you loved and how
you loved and everything you gave and everything
you did in this place is an amount, a sum and you
can see everything that you did and it is final and it
is an amount, a sum and it counts and is never
modified by what comes after, in this place

(well this is 'paradise' then. it's a place that can
come anywhere in life, and where everything
counts. This is a fairytale story,
the story of a child deprived of love, (of course)
the story of a movement between two worlds,

occurring in a short poem I wrote to you in like,

July

(when I see you as you are
nothing can hurt us
and nothing is despised
time runs in any direction
the words race into me
for the first time
and everything is magnificent
forest desert ocean tundra terrain steppe cityscape
etc.)

and I could no longer avoid the question now of
how much love that was, since even if my love
should continue to grow nothing would
change)
in this place, where everything you gave and
everything you did is an amount, a sum and you
can see everything that you did and it is final and
it is an amount, a sum and it counts,

um yeah. even if it is a fairytale story
it can never be made not to count, because nothing
can be made not to count, nothing can be erased,
can, um. yeah can be erased in this place, in which
everything is visible, is final and it is a sum an
amount and it counts and what you did is what
you did and what you loved is what you loved
and how you loved and everything you gave and
everything you did in this place is an amount, a
sum and you can see everything that you did and
it is final and it is an amount, a sum and it is

like skies do. and what you did is what you did,
and what you loved is what you loved and how
you loved, and how you loved and so one day, it
counts and it counts and is visible as an amount,

as a sum and it counts um, yeah. Scary. and even if
it's just a scary fairytale story about being taken to
a place where nothing can be changed, in which
everything is visible as an amount (where what you
did is what you did and what you loved is what you
loved and how you loved and will never be modified
and will never be erased because nothing is ever
erased in this place, in which each act is an amount,
a sum and is final), you see everything in this
bathroom mirror, and you see everything counts,
and it is final

...
...

Um.

it's a fairytale story. It is the story of a child
deprived of love. Gentle, badly treated Cinderella
goes to the little tree where her mother's grave
lies, she shakes it and a beautiful dress falls down

This is the basic justification for endless

counterinsurgency, the way you continue to

You have to live with that.

On the other side of the bathroom mirror, there's
a road, with houses, trees and a few malnourished
waifs. The sky will do.

In each window, the wasted faces of angelic
children gaze down upon our

,

And along the road you can see the footprints left

by the driver's wings: that each counts only for
itself, that each is final—

this is what I brought back with me from
'paradise'. Though

the driver turns into a girl on the swing. She is
pregnant. She looks at the sky I guess. it's the
largest possible thing there is. Less expensive than
hotels. or waking in a room she doesn't recognise,
it is the story of a movement between two worlds
separated by a space of air or an impassable forest.
I guess. She looks at her phone, I guess.

(eyes closed)

    (eyes open) (eyes closed) ((are you asleep?)

      (eyes closed)

        (eyes closed)

  (eyes closed)

Another poet

    they open their eyes, they write

'The only way to write a poem in which everything counts is

you make someone else feel that they're not unique.

you address a specific fraction of them (I am beginning to find

the only way to write a successful poem is,

you make someone else feel that they're not unique (keep going).

instead of the whole of them, you address a fraction of the other person,

the part filled with the same blinding white light

it makes no sense to me but this is just how I feel about it. It's the light that appears

in you and stays there and writes poems inside you with silence which I have
    already mentioned

and that only exists in lines that make no attempt at communication,

(of the harsh overhead light of the bathroom, the pathetic, unassuming string of
    its pullcord)

and if you do it right the whole of them is visible in their faces, their mind has
    forced its way

through the membrane, reality has been shattered, has ceased to exist

as they had known it, a feverish denial is already visible in their expression

but it is too late, in the bathroom mirror something incomprehensible looks

back at them like a smashed statue in a London nobody knows of,

and—this is the only way I know how to describe it—

you both see then the thing that makes them feel

impossibly small [something incomprehensible] 'terribly unreal

stretching and folding, weightless and brief

and as I fall further and further from understanding, all I can do is keep

talking about it

…
…

just kidding

'Impossible white light'.

Just kidding.

'I write poems that won't stop coming in my mouth and feel
impossibly small.'

Reality burnt and I fell out

7 a.m., Pago brought in by the dark haired porter,
Frau something or other, you still asleep,
the ravenous consumption of bread rolls and honey
from a little carton,
the too strong black coffee,
served to me by Frau ?

who already knew how I took it, the little objects d'art and
tchotchkes from
Olia on the windowsill, the attempt to do yoga
on the bathroom floor where the
disinfectant burnt the skin
of my hands

and your new vocabulary,
ouch and please and help (such a
short word when you said it,
always rushing
towards the terminal plosive),
or our beautiful collaborative one-two-three
when I lifted you
'ready?' 'yes', 'mollify me',
'hard serviette',
and your anger at me which I will love now forever,

your fear, your wake-up call ('help'),
the li
ttle movement in your extremities,
at first just your fingers and then later
of your hands, rotations,
interlacings,

and the terrible heartrending fear and need and dependency
in the last conversation with Barscht, the way your head
moved how it turned so quickly
backwards and forwards,
my love for you my love for you,

your beautiful frightened eyes with their sudden new
yellowness,
the dream, the nightmare you described to me
about Martina Dragschitz
when she went into the department copier (was eaten?)
and you said that if the copier doesn't work then Martina
doesn't either

and you were so frightened,

and the foul dinner with the miniature sweetcorn,
the different hums, the night when I thought you were crying
out in pain
but you were just humming to yourself quietly,
in the dark

which I connect now with your apologising,

for humming in your flat all those years ago
when you were worried I thought it would sound childish,
the humming at night which happened after you were there
with Zoe and Larne and Dimitra,
after the conversation where you said you had never had a
relationship like ours,

that had lasted so long, that you had nothing to compare it to,

and I said that you were the meaning of intimacy for me, that
intimacy was just you,
and you said you would keep loving me long after you were
gone
and I cried and I cried,
and you said you would haunt me   (the day Alexi visited),

and after your last breath, the moment when I walked back in
on you
and started, twice,
thinking at first that there was someone else in the room
and then that it was a corpse
and only then that it was you   (why were we
leaving you behind

there then we were
alone
together and I could kiss you briefly on your open lips, and
stroke your hair, and kiss
your forehead that I have kissed so many thousands of times
and two days before, after I'd taken you to the toilet at 3.30 a.m.

when we finally got back to the bed
—the last time this happened at night—
when you said
'I love you', still sitting on the side of the mattress, having
gotten through the ordeal
one last time, one last time and all the times I said I love you,
ich liebe dich, I love you,

and kissed you on the lips,

and the way that afterwards when the disbelief and the wish to
stop living had been exhausted there was still gratitude beneath
it, bottomless, calm, endless gratitude, more of it than I could
ever express or exhaust or disturb imperturbable and grey and
flat like a sea and spreading outwards in every direction, as
though it were the substance of everything else, and no wind
(only the sound of the words repeating

Acknowledgements

A first draft was performed at a reading with Wendy Lotterman at Stichting Perdu in November 2024.
    With thanks to Marija Cetinić, to everyone at Perdu, to Wendy and Phil, for everything.

Published in 2026 by The Last Books, Amsterdam
www.thelastbooks.org

Copyright © 2026 by Danny Hayward

Designed and typeset by Phil Baber
Printed and bound in the Netherlands by Wilco

ISBN 978-94-91780-85-1